Masculinity Parable

Poems by

Myles Taylor

Masculinity Parable

ISBN: 979-8-9878871-7-2

Cover design and layout by Hannah Gaskamp.

Edited by Alex Everette and Josh Savory.

Formatted by Josh Savory and Myles Taylor.

www.gameoverbooks.com

one

two

three

something in my veins / bloodier than blood
-Wilco

one

poem of only lies

I was the bad boy in school, necked in shoplifted silver & drugstore nails.
Watched horror flicks under bad fleece.
Started smoking in high school until I got smart.
I get smarter as I age & know it.
I do something feminine and a chorus calls it *big dick energy*.
I hang out in the local guitar shop.
The cashier learns my name & talks shop with me.
Every time I am good at a thing I am told I could pursue it.
I don't want to, though.
I don't take myself too seriously.
I join a dating app for other people who *don't take themselves too seriously*.
I go to a campus bar with a fake ID and laugh a lot.
I bar-hop under the stars.
I know all of their names.
On my way home I see a poster of a shirtless man in a motorcycle jacket
& I go outside shirtless with a motorcycle jacket.
My dad loves how much I look like him & hates how much I talk like him
& worries how much I act like him.
My dad grows as he ages.
Expands until he spindles like a redwood tree
& from above he calls me my name and says something about basketball.
I was born with a God that I could grow out of.
I have a dream: the shirtless man in the motorcycle jacket is in the mirror.
He opens the mirror like a car door and puts his hand on my sternum.
His hand breaks through and my chest spills sprouts of purple orchids.
I run away trailing flower petals & wedding processions begin to follow.
Two brides follow the same path of petals & collide.
I empty of flowers until I am light as a feather.
I blow away happily.
I have another dream: the shirtless model is in front of me.
He puts his hand on my sternum.
I tell him I can't feel anything & he knows.
His hand is on someone else's body.

I wake up without a body.
I wake up a man.
I wake up thinking about breakfast.
This poem never turns.
I remember why I wrote it.
I remember why I wrote it.
I remember why I wrote it.
I spend money without budgeting for future medical bills.
My chest is covered in tattoos of orchids I do not worry about butchering.
I don't go by a nickname anymore.
I use a public bathroom.
I see myself in the mirror.
I do not write this poem again.
I don't have to don't to make things true.
I never never. I always. I just do.

an explanation I do not owe

I wake up with the sun glittering onto me / my shower glitters so hard
you can hear it / I pour coffee over giant chunks of glitter
and taste the cool of it / I buy the sparkly toothpaste

so if I bleed the sink still shines / foamy prom dress mudslide
and then the morning ritual / choosing between discomfort
or discomfort / passing and passing and not passing

a mirror for a clean breath / I am thinking about the whole
futurity thing / when my favorite professor *shes* me
and it is almost like it does not happen

but I still wonder all class if skipping dinner
will make my jaw more angular / or my body more throwable
but I survive it / and do this revolutionary thing where I keep talking

talking with this voice / these bundles of string lights
caught in my throat / I am told that glitter is a feminine thing
but the closest I can get to passing for a thing
no one has a word for is to look as DIY as my name

I cover myself in glitter / because I am effectively already covered in glitter
I wear men's everything and might as well be in a ball gown / my eyes are
two giant chunks of reflective confetti / I speak / and glitter pours out of
my mouth I eat / and taste shards of glass I bind / and feel grating specks
of plastic / I walk down the street / I must be covered /
because no one can look away / but I must be so bright
they can't actually see me

If I try to be visible / I get buried in the numbers of it
it's that collection of moments that get us in the end / I'm so tired
of looking like an emergency siren / there is no surgery
for a sometimes / and if there was I would need centuries of sleep
to take back all the deep breaths I've lost /
it's like an inheritance

every trans person I know
knows a trans person who has died
and here I stand

in a room with no ghosts
waiting for a knock at the door

If Less Than A Boy is A Fruit
-Ari Banias

well let there be blueberries [let them be blueberry] spackled
the walk from the car [the vines grow so low we were so enamored
with ourselves] it took us the whole path down before we realized
jacob was climbing down the other side [the way the sun just does
its job and we say heaven] we were freezing in August we could see
which trees across the state got sunshined that day [not us]
on the way back we passed milkweed and of course a perfect garment
architectural and smooth full of goo and maybe half a wing [and how
ridiculous we were there, aweing a transition and stained blue,
being bodies no one else can see] watching over a forsaking
natural [a r]evolution [how a body can do everything in its ability
to catch up with itself] [yes I said bodies again because we are
all built] the great equalizer being my pansy knees [which requested
instead a photoshoot by the vines] I am unafraid to pretend to be
what I know I am not without the [in][as]surance to become
while the other queers on the trail relent and we try
to look every way yes [despite the view] down has more fruit

considering top surgery, ending in a set of questions for the surgeon

I have been told / that *God doesn't make mistakes.*

     Well, she sure made you. / And my ex. And brains

connected to hands. / Hands that can flatten

and morph. Build a body / out of stitch and mesh

and brains that can say *this*. / Brains, connected

to whatever this is / we call *gender*

and attribute to someone else / like we didn't make this mess ourselves

at some point along the way. /

         Decide what a chest should say.

So here I am. / Saving enough money / for a televangelist vacation /

to use on a white room / and months of new pains.

Tell me: did God make entitlement? /

         Or did entitlement make your God?

Did a man turn a lump of cells / into a contract?

Or was that just me? / Am I the mistake I made? / Did I miss the directions

down the path / in all that silence?

Was his hand on me / supposed to be pointing the way?

Or was it still guiding me?

Was it meant to show me my place?

Do I still feel it at night because I know / what should not have been here in the first place?

Folks say / *God doesn't make mistakes* / but for once / I don't want to reclaim what I was given / I just want to cut that shit / off /

how can I be a traitor / to a God I've never met?

/ Who do I belong to, again? / Where'd I get all this noise from? / Why can't I just bake for the picnic? / Whose hands do I owe my old life to / before I buy a new one?

I already gave it away. / He's had it for years.

high violet

Gender and desirability are not the same
but they attend the same terrible house parties—
perhaps play king'/s and pretend they are having fun
being personified, the way I do
when others talk about body language
and signals. I don't know what it is to be desirable
because I don't know anything other than desire.
I just want. My gender is negative space
around a want I can't even make out the shape of
sometimes, a smoked line, a Microsoft Paint-level
gradient. I'm trained in figure drawing, you know.
A pencil is a shitty reference point unless it's the only thing
you're holding. Sometimes my cat screams at nothing for hours.
We do everything he asks of us and nothing will satisfy
his cursed wails. I wish I could express myself in a similar fashion
but I think someone would probably call an emergency service.
I fantasize about loss of control and like
maybe trying bondage one day and then
I put on a weighted blanket and lost my shit.
I like the idea of everything but everything in practice
is terrible except any night I have company that can talk
as fast as me or the moment I am eating a very good meal.
I want so much more than other bodies
but one feels more doable than the others. In theory.
In practice, relinquishing control is deciding
my body and mind are not worthy of their time.
This is the only self-love I've figured out how to employ
other than a face mask. Every time I get hungry I feel like
the world is going to end. I am in control of everything I do,
I just make a point of being stupid sometimes to allow myself
a wider range of options. I only want to die
when I'm holding in a feeling
or putting thoughts in other peoples' minds.
I never promised to be reasonable.
Get this thing off of me.

The Masculinity Parable

My dad loves to earn the trust of skittish animals.
For every happy puppy in the world he finds
the cats with trust issues and makes them
a project. A local dog was afraid of men
due to a violent past but one day
she poked her thin nose into his palm.
He's taught the cat to jump up on the bed
and soon he says he'll pick her up and she
will learn something from him, or maybe he
will feel like a beast worthy of breath.

I am checking in on a man who does not
check on others. I am waiting for him
to ask me any question. I say I am not
in love with him I am just desperate
for an equity of care. For love to be reward
means there is life after the ceremony,
where it sits on your mantel, and maybe
you get around to polishing it, here and there.

If God Gave A Fuck About Trans People They Would've Made Us Crabs

or some other creature with transient body—
often I look in the mirror and think, I want
this self to live on, but not with me inside,
a donation cusping the crest of a tiny wave
that may display it for a test-run. I admit,
I like my birth name, catchy for somebody else
to take. My figure is a pretty thing to waste.
The gender therapist descriptions talk about
finding who you really are. I think I'm a few
different people. I email them anyway. Say
If I could leave my titties on the side of a beach
for some beautiful woman in need to discover
I think we'd be more of a Capital C Community.
Just saying. I don't think God is taking notes
but it would be cool if they were. I want a lineup
of striped shells. I want to shout into each
and pick the best echo, like the voice
wailing a tune that makes me cry
in front of the Uber driver. I keep busy
so a therapist can't disappoint me.
I don't want to have my body changed.
I want to leave it for somebody else to find.

craigslist -> boston -> volunteers

☆ paid antidepressants research study
☆ bipolar disorder study PAID
☆ Do you have a drinking problem?
☆ ARE YOU TRAPPED BY DEPRESSION
☆ paid transgender smokers study
☆ Is Your Teen Depressed Or Anxious?
☆ paid: drink alcohol and watch TV
☆ Trauma exposed adults needed
☆ do you have a drinking problem?
☆ do you have a drinking problem?
☆ Do you experience low mood?
☆ can you afford regular treatment?
☆ Do you lack health insurance?
☆ Does your family doctor not believe you?
☆ paid: schizophrenic patients needed
☆ struggling with memory loss?
☆ Are you so broke you're ready to use your trauma for money?
☆ Are you here because all you can do right now is scroll?
☆ is your country's medical system so broken craigslist is your only affordable treatment option?
☆ struggling with memory loss?
☆ struggling with memory loss?
☆ Anxiety Study!
☆ OCD study patients needed paid
☆ patients needed to set up a phone call 2 weeks from now and never pick up for fear that someone will tell them they aren't mentally ill they're just lazy and also an asshole
☆ are you too busy for therapy?
☆ did you spend 20 minutes at the bar 3 drinks deep trying to convince your friend that you're too busy for therapy?
☆ is scrolling craigslist the only self-care you have the energy for?
☆ PAID: depression study
☆ volunteer needed for OCD study
☆ do you want to get better?
☆ can you afford to get better?
☆ do you have time to get better?
☆ are you trapped by depression?
☆ struggling with memory loss?

A Woman Has A Theatrical Breakdown
In Front Of Wonder Bar, Allston, 2019

I think I envy her—how she can crouch and rise
in those stilettos and that bodycon dress

as she writhes, screaming, at a man who,
supposedly, always ruins everything

I think I wish I could just let it out
& make a fool of my Capricorn sensibilities

shout at the sky & sob at the glassed ground,
the McD's wraps and cigarette butts

I couldn't pick her out of a crowd
in the daytime and I wonder if she knows,

calculated the anonymity beforehand,
all red dye and bad eyeliner,

or if it's this city's timing & grace, like it's
holding her hair back, saying, alright, just this once

Aubade with Fake Blowjob

after Sam Rush

Perhaps fake is the wrong word, but there it is: Imitation.
Copy. Counterfeit. My dick is counterfeit. Sometimes silicone,
fingernail, or exhale. But in morning light, anything missing

is erased by sunbeam, maybe, or half-sleep stupor, eyesight
dizzied with lovelorn dreams. My eyes close & my whole body
might be misremembered. Put the covers where I don't want

to believe. The only un-lies in this room: you
& the light, and what, tell me, is the difference?
Your mouth & the sun? Illumination & creation?

Some people want us to change, & some people
show us what we want to be & how we have already
become it. Dick of halogen. Fluorescent silence.

The sheets, humility. The curtains, liars. The moan,
distortion. This town, sepulchre. Your spine, a vision.
The sun, marble. Your mouth, a sculptor. Your mouth,

a tool. Your mouth, a blade. Your mouth, white-hot
heat welding my and self together. Melt my two bodies
into one blinding shudder. Give shape to what I've named.

My body, museum of empty frames. My body, taxidermy
of the still-alive. My body, admittedly, small, but still all mine,
and you don't mind. Your hair, my gravity. You, gravity.

You, everything the light tumbles towards. You tell me
afterwards that it was ethereal. As if the light
wasn't all yours. The brightness stains in quiet.

Shadows stripe the little-known. You glow. You always
glow. You lightbulb a vision of myself, where your eyes
are everyone's eyes. Where the heat comes with the light.

The Line

I hate the way I feel when the boss laughs at something I say.
I make fun of an overeager applicant and they smile
like the transformation is complete. The toxic in my masculinity
is a twenty dollar bill soaking like a teabag.

—

My gender is kitchens. The slang of a lunch rush
and harsh quips that only go skin-deep. I think
of my friends who sling drinks and skate
past a crowded counter. I see the camaraderie

over an experimental meal. I picture wild acts of hubris
to flip an egg. Leading my hand into a rosetta.
I learned to be a man behind a bar, a line, a storefront.
I learned to be a man by being unafraid of flames,

for other people to get fed. Nothing makes me feel more
like a man than nurturing
a stranger.

—

I want to burn down every chain restaurant
and let the people take over. If I come into work sick
I want to get sent home without sacrificing wages.
If a customer treats me like a Roomba we take his picture

and put it on a DO NOT SERVE wall. If my knees are acting up
I want to take an extra break. I want customers to want to know me
as well as I know them. I want to push tables aside to make
a meeting space. I want to push them further out

to make a dance floor. I want to adapt to the moment.
I want to be loud and political on the clock. I never want to serve

another fucking cop again. I want health care that could cover
my transition and any job-related injuries. I want a workplace

that doesn't romanticize injury.
I still want to trade burn marks with the cooks, I just want them
to be healed properly. I want to invite everyone I know
to visit me, and I want to make them something special, on the house.

—

When I find a boss who can handle me, it's a miracle.
But they leave. And when they leave, I say goodbye
to the rest of the staff. Prepare my resume. The others say
they won't let any bullshit happen, they'll fight for me,

but I've been through this a million times.
Trans-competent bosses are so rare, I never get two
in a row. I work and work and try to stay gentle
and pull my muscles and wreck my body because

I find a boss that sees me as a human first,
a guy second, and there is no third. The bar
is on the floor of the basement office. I become
what they want me to be, a man who wants to make money,

a hard-edged non-stop, I sharpen until I am nearly
too thin to see, and as soon as they shape me into something
they can respect, they leave.

—

In the movie Ratatouille (yeah I know), a rat risks his life
to cook for people who want to kill him. He makes no wages
because the rat world has no need for money.
If food remained an art, we would still want to make it.

—

I tell everyone I am having a good time
working at a nightmare instagram tourist trap
because my coworkers think I deserve basic rights
and decency. I serve rainbow sprinkles

and try to throw up my own in the bathroom.
I stare at food all day and starve myself.
My mental health is at its bottom tier.
I stay because my coworkers call me the right pronouns.

—

Capitalism is the antithesis of tenderness.
Makes respect a scarcity for marginalized people
so it can be monetized. Makes empathy
an unachievable sales goal. Being trans

in the workplace means clocking in one day
and finding out you might not be yourself
in two weeks. The bar is too heavy to lift
after putting away the delivery.

If I didn't have to sell my body's labor
I wouldn't need it to be called anything
in the first place. What is masculinity
without capitalism? Sitting down?

—

Perfecting my avocado spread.
Being taught what to salt:
tomatoes, strawberries.
Making my first latte heart
before snapping on the plastic lid.

I MAKE A JOKE ABOUT BEING
TOO PUNK FOR THIS PLACE

and the security guards
laugh.
Thankfully.
These two men
at the entrance,
fixture beyond
bulletproof glass.
Sea-foam desk
& heavy
door leading on.
They have asked
me to empty
my pockets
of metals & my
leather jacket's pins
and zippers light
the wand up like
a strobe,
like a car
alarm, like the beat
of a song
I would've hated
in high school.
But I made them
laugh, &
they let me
pass.

And yes,
before this was
the procession—
the men
with signs.
Ripped up babies,
bloody and
botched,

lots of *red*,
red,
red I
am taking steps
to stop seeing
each month. Red
like the states this
supposedly only
happens in. Men
with signs. Then
a security desk
then a metal
detector then
a heavy door
then a sticker
on the wall
designating
BOMB THREAT PROCEDURE
the same cheap labels
my job uses to distinguish
our teas.
The receptionists
are too kind,
impossibly patient
to have seen
what I just saw
every day
and not lose it,
men with signs,
wrecked fetuses,
bad photoshop,
disapproving Jesus,
signs that say they heal
the wrong way.

The part that matters
less. People
that matter less.

They ask
if it is safe to use
their employer's name
on the telephone.
They offer to
put things in
blank envelopes.
I want to shake
someone. I want to
kick things over.
I want to say,
this is a doctor's
office. This shouldn't
be normal.

This is her normal.

She asks me why I'm here.

Whatever comes out
of my mouth could be

I am here to look more like the people you are protecting yourself against

and when she pulls
out the paperwork,
she sees I already
have a pin with the pink
and white P's, and she
thanks me, so genuinely,

this pin that proved
itself to not be
a weapon. Reader,
I am a fool.
Planned Parenthood is the most punk rock place in the world.
She walks through
a metal detector.
She looks at a bomb
threat procedure.
She heals people
who no one else
will heal.
& when I take
that form,
I decide,
if I am here
to be anything,
it's those guards
at the entrance.
& I wonder what
their stories are.
If this place saved
their wife
or sister
or girlfriend or partner
or child or boyfriend
or them or if they were just
raised right or if there really are
just two good men in this
world. I wanna say,
if there are no good men,

I'm gonna make one;
myself.

two

THIS SUMMER HAS THE POTENTIAL TO BE MIRACULOUS

which might just be the whiskey milkshake talking but the sky
is stupid with its sunset, the most universal symbol
of beauty. No human is too good to wax poetic
about an orangepink cloud. Not even the suited
and citied and sidewalked. You can't pass the Charles
in his new dress without smiling and missing your stop.
So I'm a nature bitch now. I'm in a lover's quarrel
with the Prue. I've got eyes like a real man
& the stores close too early to catch me.
I walk past the fat dandelions on my way home
and don't even check what handmade structures
wound up penthouses for rats.
I know like a hundred people with jackets
and most of them love me. My dad is always
sending me pictures of clouds so I send him
weird band names off the Allston streets
and neither of us talk about feelings. A bug
liked the looks of my phone screen while I
wrote this. I told her she was looking
at the wrong kind of light.

Fill

Nearly hollowed by the rough dig
of a dry-swallow, my throat—
countless forced chalks, handfuls of ibuprofen
before I was told the headache was not
an ache at all, but a fire drill, a growth
only the lexapro could knee. The acne pills
as well, friends squirming at their size,
but I was well practiced, they dropped in
dragging throat cells like DNA found under
fingernails. This is all to contextualize the doctor's
confusion when I, who happily thread needles
into my fat to put the boy in me, who spend all
this time filling with medicine, admitted
I could not handle a blood draw. *But you're so
good with needles*. It has never been about
the sharp, it's about the loss. The way my body
hoards whatever I lend it. I collect, you see.
I can control the accumulation, but the exiting,
the removal, is a greater unknown. I am a superstore
inside with a built-in pharmacy. Raised by hoarders,
born of always lesser possession. Not a temple
because nobody else is allowed inside, not even the nurse
who taught me how to inject the testosterone. I did
my first shot myself before she could get out a word.
I am a beloved first vehicle. A meticulous bedroom.
I consume and I fill. I tried it once,
okay? I did. Bad enough where the blood
dripped. And I saw it on the carpet and decided that
was the last time. Because that was mine. I put a lot
of work into that blood. So yeah, I absorb like
a pumice stone. I eat frighteningly healthy.
I hold my body like the only one I'll ever get.
I tell myself it will be okay and I believe myself.
I believe myself when I am asking myself,
alone, to take.

Meditation on Control

I have a crisp white shirt for any day of the week.
I have a bag full of things other people do not.
There's a thick slice of heirloom tomato at the bottom
of everything I make. I'm still getting eight of pentacles
in every draw so the world makes sure I don't stop
being ridiculous. I am a boy perpetually chiseling.
Pentacles have many meanings, but everyone keeps
conflating them with capitalism. I'm just trying to make stuff
without some water sign telling me to relax.
Magic is the agreement that something is meaningful.
I want the corner of magic and structure.
I want a miracle that I've made.

My Dentist Tells Me I Have Abnormally Large Nerves

and I wonder if that applies to the rest of my body. Every illness unexplained by nurses' shrugs, all overgrowth. The headaches through childhood due to an abnormally massive brain—not in the intelligence sense, just a lotta room in there, an echoing mansion-brain with a foyer skylight shattered by the tight skull loomed outside. My knee problems in high school from big joints swollen against their caps. I was fitted into too small a skeleton. My marrow pushes me up into a constant sprint. My eyes, my ears, ill-fitted parts I'm not smart enough to name. The TMJ comes from the nerves trying to escape their chokehold. Would my veins have broken from the pressure if I hadn't occasionally drained them in youth? Maybe my heart is literally too fucking big. Maybe expected, but so what. Maybe the raw rip of my fear, the confused burn, is my heart trying to break out from between two too-big lungs. I don't even know if these are metaphors. To be unaware of the state of your own body is a deeply American thing. Refusing treatment of pain I can bear was my first lesson in American masculinity. Mystery illnesses growing into me, then growing on me. Doctors have fully fucking shrugged because I couldn't afford further investigation. And now I'm finding out my wreck of a mouth is full of huge literal nerves. I paid four hundred dollars and left.

Second Puberty

I know my teeth are sharpening but just pretend they're
little candy corns or slips of paper I've swallowed
to keep secrets. Let's say yours. When I come
back it's like I've blacked out. I hate when I leave
myself. I found my face on a spoiled carton.
I met myself up on a flagpole. What the fuck,
God? People keep asking me *how are you?*
But I can't even answer the *who* so how
am I supposed to make it past the W's?
I mostly know *when*. Hell if I know *why*.
Which ones am I missing? Whatever. What's
new? Festering, thanks. Photosynthesizing.
Sinking into a cushion. You ever get
a Grindr message without remembering making
a profile? It's the T-shot blues, everyone
clap along. Thought I had a grip on myself
but I slipped right out again. I feel like a showgirl
bursting out of a cake, every time. How am I?
Mostly I'm just that moment
after some excitement, a vacation,
a birthday party, where you just feel the air
cup your body as it settles into the after,
and you reach wrist-first into your chest,
pulling heartbeats back out.

My Therapist Tells Me I Can Cry
And I Tell Her I Already Did Last Week

My friend says he's figured out who he is,
he just doesn't like the guy. I know about love.
I know what to do with it. I know how to go
about my day. I shell chickpeas at work
and watch their ghosts float out of the bowl.
I work food because I am good at it.
Lifting a heavy thing is entirely willpower if you don't
care about your body. My body knows more about love
than I do because I keep making eye contact with the same
people. They talk about some people needing to make
their own mistakes, which is why I don't learn things.
I'm not charming enough to suck. I learn to wink.
I collar grief and eat the leaves left on the line. I think
I can lift 22 quarts of water. The phrase *feeling empty*
is a red herring because water is clear. I couldn't do it
until I could.

Unskilled Labor

Behold my barber's gilded scissors, a gift
from a loyal client. Look at the planning, the economy,
of the razors on hooks the barber's height,
the best ones worn-handled, their storage trunk
scattered with stickers of old bands resting
in dead iPods in coffee table drawers. Come with me,
to the street. Watch the house painter's pants
match every few buildings he passes, as if the city
were trying to copy them. Watch your morning barista
pull a rosetta without looking. Peek in the shop windows,
admire every crisp fold the floor staff creased into every
shirt, watch the quick wrist of the window-washer,
witness the wrangling of the dog-walker's five leashes,
the two-part movement of the city worker sticking litter.
Come into my restaurant! Admire the server
and their patient smile. Plant two knocks on the kitchen door,
shout *in*, and bear witness: line cooks seasoned
with years of oil and salt, working so smooth
they've made it a dance. Clogs two-stepping while sauce
whips the dish, the sous milly-rocking a metal bowl
into the bus bin, the bang of the skillets to clear
the crusted rice in time with the beat from the phone
propped into the metal six-pan on top of the reach-in.
See a hand reach back and be given a spatula
it didn't ask for. Watch the dishwasher replace the glasses
in the blink of an eye while she FaceTimes her niece.
It looks nothing short of telepathy, the slide
through narrow spaces like wrong sides of magnets,
all of which have a knife. And still conversation flows:
who just sold a sculpture, who has a paper
to write, who's playing a show later, who was up
until 4 am at their other job, performing a whole
different dance, a symphony of second-nature
movements, muscle-memorized like their country
is a fatigue mat and they have mapped every corner.

I only dream of labor if I can make it beautiful,
so I slice every scallion like a gift-wrap ribbon and roll
my eyes at every customer who taps their foot.
Skill is love. Do you? Love? Show me yours.
Your skill. Walk me through your day and allow me
the scenes I won't see. I want to see your method
for cleaning a bathroom the quickest. Your filing system.
Your best customer service voice. Or do you go home
to a sparkling kitchen someone else cleans,
eat food someone else cooks, watch shows
someone else writes? Do you use programs
someone else codes, attend meetings someone else
schedules? What do you do?
You take. And you hold what you take.
What a skill, being handed things. Such talent
in holding.

The Patron Saint of Retail Speaks

I heard you speaking to your knotless and well-therapized
friends about *listening to your inner child.* I know the child
well. She does not speak, though. She points.

She feels the swell of possible worlds in every book store.
Spirits in mall windows whisper, *you deserve this.* And she does.
And so do you, I think. Any glitter that catches

the corner of the eye, any shirt that announces
who you are and what you like. I like your inner child.
The voices of humans are grating on my ears. But this child

knows when to be quiet. This is the child who hid under a coffee table
for an hour, clutching a Hello Kitty figure with a strawberry
for a head, praying her parents would give up searching and go home.

Leaving you in your classmate's mansion. Leaving you to keep
the strawberry cat. Thinking, *she won't notice. She already has
all of this. If I had all of this, I would give it out like candy.*

When did you connect the dots? When did you realize
it was not cool or fun to be afraid of the future? That your friends
lived in an entirely different world? See, here, under this table,

she still thinks she is the protagonist of the young adult novels
she started reading too early, the grown genius orphan,
the poor kid turned Chosen One, waiting to be Chosen.

You had to go through hardship, the books said, before you become
interesting. But the hardship should be over by now, she thinks,
and that's when she began to point. You are fully grown

and properly gendered and make good money and still
have the five bone-thin fingers when you do not make good money.
The child has learned to reach through you, her digits

splitting yours lengthwise like two bullseye arrows splintering
each other in the fight for highest prize. And you are peeled
and relenting by now, scrupulosity abandoned to the big,

intense eyes of this child, the unnatural fingers, and she takes
the necklace she wanted, she carries the designer shoes,
she enters your credit card number into the little box.

The eyeliners fall in your pocket. The barcodes scan for two.
The sunglasses stay in the shirt collar. She has read every
spy novel and employs their tactics with relish. In a poem

you lied that you were a bad boy once. Badness
is non-applicable in a system that relies on the evil
of currency. I did not ask for capitalism, it just happened

and now the people flock to me like a possession
could hold their grief for them. It cannot.
But you know that. You're not stupid. The girl,

she is not stupid. You have just run out of alternatives.
Retail therapy is a harm reduction strategy,
you think, but whose harm? Which harm, and where?

There is so much and only two of you. Where
is the strawberry cat now? Did she keep it?
Do you even remember?

Smol Bean

...that's me! I'm a smooth joint down there,
a blank box you can draw a kitty in. See?
Look at all the puns I'm good for. Witty remarks
in a pair of shorteralls. My calling card
is an x somewhere it isn't needed.
Gender is a performance and I'm typecast
in all the teen dramas. My baseball cap says
#1 Dad and it is funny because I am so soft
and so small and a dad cannot be soft nor small
nor smooth nor feminine in any form. I must
be a student somewhere. Either that or a slur,
I guess, so I'll take it! Be bad at everything
women supposedly are. Play ukulele. Swallow
my sex drive. Manic pixie genderfuck.
Sexuality is a beast and gender is a chinchilla.
The golden oil ate me alive. The moment
my voice dropped I spat out my own bones.
Sprouted like a werewolf. Once it got hard
to be cute I got a lot less valid. I'm still not a man,
yet. But oh god, there's a pair of eyes in the dark.

Suit of Cups, or A Queer Love Story
In Various Bodies (of Water) *after Franny Choi*

Jones Beach		Endless blues scare the shit out of me. Oceans are more powerful than anything a human frame can make. I learned about riptides in grade school and that was that on that.
Paint Cup		You see any river and ask it your body. I ask the ground my body and I keep getting the sky. The ocean knows too much to be trusted.
The Merrimack		I told you *I don't think it's that kind of river* and you didn't believe me until we passed it and its steep rocks for ourselves & man do those waters have somewhere to be
The Charles	x	I told you *I don't think it's that kind of river, like the Charles,* and you looked at me like I thought I could hold the rain. I thought about every lonely pass through Kendall, how I'd look across the Prue lights reflected and think, *it's all mine. This whole city is mine.* How wrong I was. This city's sequined sash, all yours.
That Night	x	I got all over my own futon and still you stayed for hours pressed over me like a wave encased in a blanket which I guess is what we all are: water with a big soft glove, trying to press into things without losing parts of us in the process
Sebago Lake	x	I floated out to the rope and back. I'm in love with you.
Our Shower	x	The sensory hell of your light/fan situation is over. The day after you move in there is a plant behind the curtain. I ask if we need dirt so close to where we clean ourselves and you said it needs a lot of moisture to live and this is where I remember how many living things you keep thriving in this house. In this world. You took it out but now I want it back.

If You Think Bodies Are Static
You Have Clearly Never Had Queer Sex

We all have Google, I know: If a tree falls in a forest, it doesn't make a sound
because sound is made in each of our ears from vibrations. Feeling, similarly,

requires the nerves to happen. So if half of my body dissociates
every time. If I imagine our legs otherwise. If my eyes stay open

but I feel something other than what I see. What is that?
Facts and reality are two different things. Reality is just a lot of people

agreeing. Months of injections from now, a group of people might see me
and the reality of me will be a whole lot different than the fact of it.

*In between & all kinds of whole and unembarrassed tonight, gin-dazed
and asking to be both the hips and the knees, for submission to submission.*

If two people at night decide there is a dick between them
and no one else is there to see it, are they wrong?

And can you prove it? If the only people in the room know
what they feel. If our nerves go rogue against the night.

*I am not the kind of guy who likes to ask for directions.
Soften me. I am a muscle used too often to know how to stretch.*

if I look in their eyes and see it, is my dick a mass hallucination?
A conspiracy theory? Every ghost story involves somebody

who'll go to their grave believing what they saw, whether or not
there's a rational voice they're ignoring, or maybe listening to,

but they can't shake it, this tendency to doubt. I'm not doubting the ways
my pleasure comes to me. I want to believe. Queering reality is deciding

the options we get aren't good enough, and doing something about it.
I am feeling the kind of too much I am supposed to want but often get too scared

to look in the eye but today I think, I trust them, I trust them, and the world
can shatter without glass getting anywhere near my skin, your skin, our skin.

So yeah, sex with me might haunt you. Why be born right when you
can manipulate consciousness, shimmer like a fact in an age

without image, age like a document pressed between two books,
the millimeter of possibility you feel in the back of your chest

when a shape passes the corner of your eye in the middle of the night.
Trying to explain why all my loved ones are trans is hard

when you just weren't there. There, in the room of your brain
you might not have gone into yet.

SSRI Withdrawal

A recurring obsession I have involves denouncing my former selves. So sometimes I'll go out in my brain to try and kill them. The teen who hadn't read the right books yet wasn't at marching band practice, so I moved up to the college student, who had already left the show where they laughed too loud. I almost caught myself in one of the many classrooms full of my misinformed comments, but I lost myself in the crowded hallway. I finally found myself in my twenties, clocking into the job I thought I was bad at, writing all this gender drama and broadcasting all these neuroses and just generally being a menace. We locked eyes while I raised the pistol but we were both so busy being afraid of each other I didn't realize the gun was made of chalk and oil, a clean white light. I couldn't pull the trigger anyway. I looked Photoshopped, like a collage cut-out. Belonging nowhere. I looked so fucking scared. Shame is just an attempt to disown a moment you learned from. I left myself there, knowing I'd be back.

Perry Ellis

She only calls me M now,
which is about ⅓ a miracle.
She brings me into the store,

another half. Buys me a shirt
size small and my dad size large,
says he can get his for Christmas.

We say nothing. Just like a boyhood:
not needing to be explained.
She doesn't get the pronouns but

the hesitation is enough of a name
somehow. The saying nothing
about the Starbucks cup, the let's go,

M, and onwards, and really,
it's all a grasping on to what I had
and what I can get. I can write

about how much I love my family
and how much I yearn for a little
more patience at the same time.

I'm not telling you a violence. My gender
back home is my mother's face
when she realized what she said.

It is trying, and loving anyway,
moving every which way, each time
a surprise.

I Get A Day Off

so, I'm sitting on some glass-strewn rocks out back
listening to my skin eat the sun, ready to return it
to my love's arms all warm and buzzy, when I realize,
as I often do, how conspicuous I am. Always,
since girlhood, doing some weird shit in public.
Sitting down wherever I wanted, throwing
sticks around the nature trail talking to myself
at a fairly mature age. Blasting Marvin Gaye
on the front stoop of this apartment building I rent
maybe one-thirtyeighth of, acting like it's mine
for just one morning. Conspicuous enough
until I speak a kindness to a neighbor
passing my impromptu vibe session and it hits me
how the new low voice contrasts the sundress,
and, like that, conspicuous changes
into danger, or, potential danger as the medicine
shuffles my cells into shining new arrangements,
and the world prepares a new constitution for my
broadening shoulders. This is what I've asked for,
after all—paid money for, even—comfort around
loved ones, and confusion around everyone else.
The new smells like a shallot in a pan,
welcoming me home to my new body. Constantly
asking, *what the hell is that?* And that is me!
Flirting with a girl at the show before realizing
my frame could assume a threat. My threat
assuming a frame. My self more of a statement
than I know to speak so far. Hoping my sun-dressed
legs don't walk somewhere they can't leave.

poem envisioning the opposite of violence

I chop vegetables to fry & the knife slices a thin stripe of red on my finger. I twist the cut off like a wedding band & leave the new-formed ring on the side of the sink. The hot pan presses into my hand & the pink mark washes off with soap. The meal goes into my stomach and I do not regret it. Here, every car stops inches from last-minute crosswalks. A person sees a different person on the train & is filled with a steady joy. Our legs touch on the seats & we cannot imagine a reason to pull away. The train operators can afford their rent. The tracks know no blood. No one is sure what blood looks like, only we all have it, therefore we are all very fond of it. Here, we take the shortest route home at night. We pack flashlights but no knives. We do not consider our knuckles. I peel off the bruises on my knees before every work shift. The bird face-down in my driveway is taking a nap. Nothing dies here until it is ready. My uncle slipped down the stairs & the carpet plushed up to catch him. His head closed as soon as it opened. He was never a violent man to begin with. I do not have to sit here contemplating whether the death of a violent man is more violence, or less. I do not have to be the authority on violence to protect myself. Here, nobody thinks I invented the word *trigger* for fun. No one knows what a trigger is here because there are no guns here. I reach my love's bed unsore & untired. Our two bodies form the shape of the y in yes and our mouths finish the sentence. Yes and no are complete sentences. No one has ever left a fingerprint on either of us. The bird wakes up before us & sings us into morning. I stumble out to the kitchen & find the thin red ring still sitting on the counter. I slip it back on because it is mine now. All of my scars are white pearl bracelets lining my limbs. They are mine now. I dress myself in everything that has happened to me. I can remove them at any time because they are mine now. My love comes out at the smell of breakfast. Neither of us feel too small to nourish ourselves. Our bodies have no evidence of the night before. We are not afraid of this. We are never afraid.

three

Three Years

So here is the simple truth: I was a girl until I wasn't. I was a wasn't until I was. What I was, then, had to be a boy. But that isn't very helpful. The simple truth: I lead with the negative. I lead with non-ness, who I am not yet, where I will not be, what I do not have. All I can call myself is not. A knot. A knot can either tie two things together or cause a problem. Being a boy is easier. And I am one. Until I am under flashing lights or fluorescents or another man. What am I then? I identify most with the knots in my shoulders. The manliest thing about me is my hesitation toward being fixed. How could anyone use me, then? I am knot the man I have grown into. I am knot the girl I was when I learned my body. A professional asks *how are you doing?* so I pick at the first thread I see. I don't know what sits at the center. I am a rubber band ball that can't remember what I built myself around. I identify, I suppose, with being a problem. I empathize with them – the clumps at the bottom of my backpack, the strangers in my jean pocket. The amalgamations of straw wrappers and pins and pencil lead. They have greeted each other warmly, built rapport, made love, became a new being entirely, one with so little use we can only deem it trash. Is gender trash? I mean, yeah, but that's not the question. The question is, does it need to be? And this is where we start the work. Because it might be. And who will love me if it is? When I am untangling my headphones on the bus, I survey the puzzle. I consider leaving it as it is, a mess, an anti-usage. I breathe deeply. I pull.

poem with only a little bit of sacrilege

I wanna be like the heroes in the movies
but every time I drop something I jump out of the way /
I feel like the parrot in the back of my neighborhood pet store
that is obviously a mob front, like, I just keep seeing
unspeakable horrors but I can only repeat the same few words
and none of them really encapsulate my feelings / god
is a girlboss who keeps promising me a raise
and I really don't want to know how the clothes are made /
this is why I'm not in therapy / I've been too good for too long,
I need an anti-therapy / terrible advice and a couple bad influences
perched on my shoulders / let my chaos expand until I implode
into a rebirth / every day will feel like the summer I slept
on seven used mattress pads stacked on someone else's floor /
my friend brought coronas as a housewarming even though it most
certainly was not a house / nothing ever feels like a house anymore
/ I want to be a house
/ single-unit, walled and self-sustaining
/ like the moon! / like the fucking moon /
no like don't even start with me a man stumbled past me post-shift
last sunday waiting for a train that never comes and the moon was full
and the sky was clear and the man was incoherent yelling *stinky!* over
and over until he looked up and crystal clear went *oh, the moon.*
and that's the power of the moon, baby! / an all-ages event!
a birthday party! / stop writing about the moon,
boring people yell, and the poets pick up pitchforks
and yell an indistinguishable battle cry / we clash /
but no one gets hurt about the moon / truly what else
can I live for when all I see out of my window
is a car dealership and oppression
and the moon? the fucking moon
/ just good vibes and one piece
of American trash / just like me

The Trans Panic Defense is a legal strategy asking a jury to find that a victim's gender identity is to blame for and therefore excuses the assailant's actions. This is still legal in 42 states, and used in 3 ways.

1. Insanity or Diminished Capacity: news of the victim's gender identity caused the assailant a nervous breakdown resulting in violence

    which was debunked by the APA a full forty years before transgender
    was taken out of the DSM. So: the assertion that insanity
    is contagious? Or that there's a few kinds of insanity,
    and only one deserves treatment. Our eyes meet on the crosswalk.
    The uncanny valley breaks your ankle on descent.
    Mass hysteria population one. The hormones fogged your vision.
    You can't fathom this much power in a person, and you've never really
    had a thought before? So you mistake the neurons firing
    for madness. Let's talk about madness. About panic.
    I don't know any of us who do not pray
    to a pill every night, with smooth forearms and even breaths.
    Hatred is a diminished capacity, and we are always
    the affected. And let me define affected. I mean not leaving
    the house some days for fear of eye contact. If panic can cause violence,
    how are you always the safe one? Which brings us:

2. Provocation: The victim's identity provoked the assailant

    despite straight men provoking me all my life.
    I have been provoked in malls.
    I have been provoked in parks.
    I have been provoked on the sidewalk.
    I have been provoked outside of my dorm as a minor.
    I have been provoked in school.
    We have been provoked in bars.
    We have been provoked at gas stations.
    We have been provoked at our places of work.
    Explain why I have never killed anybody.
    Explain how there are enough men alive today to fill a courthouse
    or, even, a jury. Or is murder another men's club?
    Is that why you won't call me my name?

3. Self-Defense: the victim's identity caused the assailant to believe them capable of harm

–don't you get it? If we were vengeful by nature,
you'd all be dead. There's reason enough.
When one is born to a fork in the road that says
pain or *liability* you just do what you can
to get by.
Pay it no mind.
When you're born to a country that says
free for some of you, you just tire yourself out
trying to stretch definitions. Letting friends
crowd on your couch, daring landlords to talk.
Calling people family who you've just met,
because they were in front of you and said something nice.
Walking the streets in packs. Keeping your phone on
at all times just in case of an emergency and knowing
an emergency is any time your sibling needs some help
staying somewhere that doesn't want them. I don't know
a single trans murderer outside fiction written by the free
but I know a lot of dead trans people. If the law
were not a liar, we'd be the only ones left.

Ode to Cicada Shells

My favorite part was always the eyes.
Thinnest glass encasing what once navigated

such a bulbous body around bark, slow step
over textured plastic before splitting free,

leaving all that heavy on a toddler slide, or
porch beam, or well-climbed tree. I loved

in the summers, and if I loved you, you would find
a small, crinkling body attached to your sleeve.

A laugh in the dark like a firefly searching
through cupped palms. I blame nobody for angering.

Despite shouting *it's just a shell!* at the girls
I thought I was better than, different from

for the dirt under my nails, I had phobias, too.
I was irrationally afraid of the hatched versions,

their thick winged bodies and giant eyes, free
of the glass they hid behind. I wonder if they realized

they were seeing through a lens their whole lives.
I'm too tired for the rest of the metaphor. I wanted

to write a carefree poem about love and bugs
and not the boy stuck inside of them. My best friend

never fully forgave me for all the shells on the swing set.
For the layers I was born into, that I've been cracking open

one by one, rubbing my fingers against their eye sockets
and saying, *look how smooth. Look how fragile. I know*

it's scary, but look at all that un-life. How un-dangerous it could be.

Boston Poem

Everywhere there is construction.
Changing hands every three drags
to keep one warm. This is how I learn
to ask for help. I don't regret moving
to the city but sometimes I'm still
taken aback by the whole thing.
Ruining each acquaintanceship
at the first bud. Frozen Heinekens
under my porch. *Settle down*
is such a laugh. Nothing is settled
and everything is downtown.
The privileged talk about the unprivileged
like either bugs or ghosts. Sometimes
a truck still drives by blasting life
and sometimes they are singing
along, but mostly there is construction.
Everything hasn't disappeared until it has.
Settle down is what they say
when the construction is complete
and the bugs become ghosts and the ghosts
become murals on the sides of the condos.
Once the condos connect into walls,
I'll move. I'll try and no one will let me out.

For Fathers

Softness can be the base of the horns pointed down.

The you too back. Always proving you wrong,

then proving you right. Inheritance is implied.

He rambles about his psoriasis knowing you are crying

on the other end. Knees folded on the kitchen floor,

you see him in his desk chair four hours away,

that awful orange carpet, old dictionary smell.

Love does not have to be loud. How else

can you love a man who raised something

he never could have met? Won't call you your name

yet but remarks, one day, you must be the first they

to do poetry in that country.

Love is implied, everywhere.

Masculine love is a language that has to be studied.

Is the way you talk about your dying dog.

About city life. You say you're tired, and he says

you can't be a writer unless you can throw out

an entire piece & start again.

Marie Antoinette Could Not Have Said That

Shut into gilded gates with her pug puppy ripped
out of her arms, fastened into a cage around her
teen hips and draped in somebody else's dress,
you are probably already tired of this poem. It is hard,
to love a woman outlined in diamonds when you
are eating food you stole from your job before
your shift at your other job. It is hard to love
your manager when they are already glowering
when you enter the room. It is hard to love
the customer service agent on the phone.
It is hard to love. The only letters received
by Marie Antoinette from the outside world
were from her mother faulting her
for her childless womb, accusing her of repulsing
her teen husband. When something is worth hating
you are not allowed to see it. It is not clear
if Marie Antoinette was allowed to speak freely
to peasants. Marie Antoinette was given three jobs:
be fuckable, produce a son, and do not kill the son.
Making a complaint to a famous media outlet
involves two separate automated chatrooms. The CEO
of your restaurant lives in an entirely different state.
Your property owner employs a landlord employs
a property manager employs a group of men
who do not speak your language to fix the house
you live in. Hating the people I can name
has gotten boring. I want to take
a bottle of ink and douse the world until
the invisible puppeteer hands are coated
and solid and then I want to cut them off
at the wrists. I could have said douse in blood
but I do not think the ruling class has enough
blood to even tint the Atlantic ocean. There

are so few of them and they never have to leave
their houses. If you shoot messengers
and spokespeople and faces a new one will be lured
into their place with salaries and healthcare
and a new puppy. Everyone who has never said a word
to their next door neighbor is building a tiny
Versailles inside of themself.

When asked to help the poor, Marie Antoinette
did not say let them eat cake. She agreed,
and announced that Versailles will no longer buy
any more diamonds. She thought whatever amount
of their budget was for diamonds would be enough
to solve her nation's hunger.
Yes, your Majesty, was all the hands said
before turning away.

Pride 2021

Until the rats greet me back on the sidewalk
until Joan Jett can change the pronouns back in her
love songs until they put my Dunks back in the square
until I stop burning myself unidentifiable at work
until I feel loved again until I scrounge enough
favors for someone to drive me over the state border
until the dance parties come back until all my people
are freed of their obsessions with language until
I remember how to apply glitter properly until I realize
that none of it's coming back until the online wasteland
spits me out for good I'll be here in the back between shifts
just find me you know me you know where I go come
join me maybe just hold me for a second please

Old Soul

I'm teaching myself about desire. Crossing
my legs and holding my heart out like a
falcon on my wrist, nerves of the chest
sticking around it like clusters of roots,
dark and smelling of grenadine.
I'm teaching myself to live slower,
now. Stretching each step out,
extended at the leg, the way one dances
in heels at the ball, when everyone
is watching. I am feeling my blood
these days. I used to write about my body
like an attack on my brain. A Higher-Need
Sibling. My feelings blew like balloons
in my chest and I didn't trust my skin
to hold them. Junk drawer
of the body. Body of the body.
What a stupid word, with its left and right hands.
I am every part of me. No limbs
or extensions of myself are antagonists,
I am just imagining the arguments. Designing
drama like a reality TV producer. We have
a clumsy dance, an ancient rite, we work
each other like a raspberry seed stuck in teeth,
and it is beautiful under porch light. Perhaps all I need
is another's hand to show me my extent.
It is tiring, keeping track of it all. A field trip
chaperone. A glass of water too old to drink.

Boston Poem II

A lot of people talk about how hard it can be
to make a home somewhere. Romanticize the work
of uprooting & restarting. I think the hardest thing
you can do sometimes is *keep* a home.
Forgive everything it's done to you. Work with it.
Couple's counsel with it. Get fed up with it.
Let it apologize to you. Home is a safety you build
and building things takes work. I've built alone.
I've built with people. Sometimes I walk away,
sometimes they do. Sometimes it needed to be done.
Sometimes it didn't. I reflect sometimes on a mansion
I built with someone, who thought they'd run
out of rocks before they ran out of windows.
Turns out the grounds were perfect for planting.
I forgave the grounds. I eat fresh fruit and hold
sticky hands. I smile at people on the streets
who I recognize because they have seen
some secret of mine, the secret that I exist
more than once. My proudest secret.
My best structure. Kneel at your own feet
and ask them if they're tired. Kneel at the base
of your apartment building and ask the dirt
what else it's good for. If it says nothing,
keep moving. But listen first.

Suit of Wands

The intersection between service and submission. The relaxation of the muscles. The way desire points out of my chest, prickling like stalactites of the heart. The late night sore feet. The smoke in my hair. The arms flat, supporting. The intersection between support and restraint. The fold of the hand. The way even the air points to you, like my brain is leaning forward on its elbows, breathing in, like fear has decided to lie down for a while. The magnet of my trust in you could pull flecks of metal out of my skin. I live my life with a propeller on my back. You thwart inertia. I am learning allowance. You taught me.

ode to the mirror

We can see our reflections. Humans just can't see
    what we see. We become insular. The act of lonelying
is to have a myth no one will get close enough to let
    you dispel. I don't want his blood. I want something
in it. But we try so hard to be untragic
    we pick the next easiest thing.
A terror in the night.
    Reject the old silver and opt for black.
I sit wide & smoke for the rasp
    & get too bold to hide. Why do you think
I keep saying I don't gamble with sunlight.
    I keep hearing things.
I take selfies in bathrooms
    I could die in and keep doing
my makeup on the train.
    I have to limit my futures
based on where the corners
    are darkest.
No one can see me because no one is looking.

    I want to be that dramatic.
I want to say I inject
    a lineage of man into my skin
every week to stop myself
    from drinking my own wrist
but I knew I had the choice:
    to appear in everyone's backgrounds
or keep living my own kind of quiet sin
    with the rest of my species. But I know
no matter what kind of light I walk into
    I live. Even after I die.

Just some platonic choking

in jazz band, fastening the top button of a friend's thick neck,
squeezing, him promising me it would not hurt & it doesn't quite,
I think, as I pull a young boy's shirt into a chokehold
in the goodwill, the arms fitting fine but it's just that one
button, just that one, or the first I bought myself online
nineteen and looking for a mirror I could button up but not down,
not the last, being in possession of hips, so I wore it tucked
neat enough into some cutoffs with scant pockets. I am trying
to envision something fitting right, but really, I don't think
clothing is made for bodies, anyway, so maybe this fresh
scrawn is not unusual. I've been billowing all my life,
thinking of my friend's neck, how he sat
quiet ready to gag on the gender he sits in still,
that I have taken willfully, and when my dad asserts
the hormones will make me violent I touch
my narrow neck, wishing they knew
they could choose, too

There's a woman looping longhand on this train & I think,

she must be a poet. & I glance outside at the students
saddle-seated on the stone tops and I think
they must be poets, every one,
just by the look on their fresh faces at the well-placed street trees
& I look at the Boston trees and they are poets, just here to dress
the world up, right, but actually create our oxygen?
Too on the nose? The grey-haired lady on the stationary bike
absolutely going at it is a poet, no contest.
I am definitely a poet at this gym
because I have no idea what I'm doing right now.
& hark! Another poet! The trainer
speaking softly at the woman in the corner.
Every tenderness is a poet, as every tender moment,
I think, could be a poem,
& I'm leaving walking home, & the whole train line is a poet,
& my one bum knee & my one peeling knuckle,
& this one fat robin in fucking February is a poet guaranteed,
& I think my favorite poet is when my cat curls his two paws inward
like a little bowtie,
& my testosterone syringe is a poet,
& the espresso machine at my dumb job is a poet,
a poet is anything I could ask,
do you ever feel a hole in your chest?
& every time you think about it,
it rips open a little more? You ever try to fill it
with dopamine & nutrients & you are so close
to stuffing it with all the decisions you've said
you'd never make but the poets! all the poets!
Somehow they're still going, feeling the parameters
of that hole, & do you ever realize
it opened before you thought about it, you just
correlate causation, & it could be opening
further any day you are not looking at it,

Schrodinger's hole, at any size at all if you go on
about your day but oh, my poets! my poets!
Pulling it closed with two hands, I love you.
This ugly world & this uglier city. This beautiful city
& my ugly brain. You make it stop, sometimes.
I'm trying not to look but I think you do.

ANTI-ELEGY FOR ALL THE TRANS PEOPLE WHO ARE STILL ALIVE

Yeah sure, of course I've had those moments,
the ones you came here for. Holding them
while they mourn their dead trans friend,
the friend's green skin & blue gown, as if
they were simply an angel being viewed
underwater, which, you could argue,
they were, that we all are, but I don't want
to talk about that right now.
I want to talk about the moment after,
when their grief slowed & we laughed & kissed
like our bodies were actually ours
& not some too-small pillowcase our soft souls
were stuffed into, our genders muffin-topped
out the end, unprotected. I want to talk about
their laugh & her smile & their weird sense of humor
& his favorite ice cream flavor & my god,
the one that only shows up when we are crying
& only to help us hold the water back
before we find ourselves again, & then they leave,
knowing that if we have survived this long,
we can do anything they could have done
& more.

Acknowledgments

Thank you, first off, to Josh, MJ, Catherine, and the staff at Game Over Books for finally giving these poems a physical home.

Thank you to Bradley Trumpfheller, Alex Everette and Jade Kleiner for being incredible editors and/or sounding-boards.

Thank you to Lip for being my perpetual collaborator, for every stupid idea turned brilliant production, every late night adventure, every chaotic phone call. Thank you to Kels for being there for me for essentially my entire career. Thank you to Matt for anchoring me through the throes of launching this book—I love you.

Thank you to everyone who has mentored me as a poet, reader, and listener over the years, at Emerson, the Cantab, or elsewhere: Truj, Brandon, Zeke, Bobby, Kieran, Simone, Nicole, Anna, Shippy, Claudia, Dr. K, Dr. J, and probably more—it takes a village to raise a writer.

Thank you to everyone who has ever been part of the Boston Poetry Slam at the Cantab Lounge: my graduate education, my community, my home, my weird little family that I am thankful for every day. Thank you to everyone part of the Emerson Poetry Project, for showing me what I am meant to do.

Thank you to everyone who has ever been on an Emerson or Cantab slam team with me. Thank you to everyone who has ever organized with me. Thank you to everyone who has been nice to me at a poetry event. Thank you to Mrs. Petersen in 2nd grade for convincing me that I was good at this. Thank you to my family for supporting my education in a thing that was never going to make money, and for supporting me in every iteration of myself. Thank you to the weird little open mic in Oradell, New Jersey that let me yell my teenage poems between old white guys with guitars.

And thanks to the following journals for publishing poems that appeared in this book:

beestung (an explanation… & If You Think Bodies Are Static…);

The Dillydoun Review (If God Gave A Fuck…);

Crab Fat Magazine (Aubade with Fake Blowjob);

Washington Square Review (on considering top surgery…);

december mag (For Fathers & meditation on control);

86 Logic (The Line);

mutiny! magazine (My Therapist Tells Me I Can Cry…);

Academy of American Poets (poem envisioning the opposite of violence);

Underblong (THIS SUMMER HAS THE POTENTIAL…);

DEAR Journal (Suit of Cups);

Night Coffee Lit (My Dentist Tells Me…);

Faultline Journal (If Less Than A Boy Is A Fruit);

Posit (Unskilled Labor, ode to the mirror, Patron Saint of Retail);

great weather for MEDIA (high violet);

GASHER Journal (ode to cicada shells);

West Trade Review (Fill);

Up the Staircase Quarterly (there's a woman looping longhand…)

Biography

Myles Taylor (they/he) is a transmasculine writer, organizer, educator, food service worker, Capricorn-Aquarius cusp, and glitter enthusiast. They are the current Producer of the historic Boston Poetry Slam at the Cantab Lounge and former President and alum of the Emerson Poetry Project. They have represented Boston and Emerson College at the National Poetry Slam, FEMS Tournament, CUPSI, and VOX POP, and have been slamming and touring internationally for over 8 years. Their publications and performance videos can be found at myles-taylor.com, and their neuroses can be found on social media @mylesdoespoems. They live amongst the rats of Allston, MA. Masculinity Parable is their first full-length collection.